CCSS **Genre** Fantasy

Essential Question
What makes a pet special?

Polly the Circus Star

by Amy Helfer
illustrated by Judy Stead

Chapter 1

Bird-Sitting

Mrs. Ramos is going out. Bev and Ben will take care of Polly.

"Polly had her lunch," says Mrs. Ramos. "She might want a nap."

"Be good, Polly! Goodbye," says Mrs. Ramos.

"Goodbye!" says Polly. "Squawk!"

"Are you sleepy?" asks Ben.
"Do you want to nap in your
nice cage?"

"I don't want to nap," says Polly.
"I want to race! Ready, set, go!"

Polly takes off in a flash. Bev
and Ben run after her, huffing
and puffing.

Bev and Ben reach the end of the hall. The back door is open!

"Where are you, Polly?" calls Bev.

"Here I am!" calls Polly. "Come see what I can do!"

4

Chapter 2

Circus Stunts

"Look at me!" squawks Polly. "I'm in the circus!"

"Come down before you get hurt!" calls Ben.

Polly jumps from the rope and zips away. Bev and Ben run after her.

"Look at me!" says Polly. "I'm a clown in the circus!"

"You're going too fast!" says Bev. "Please stop!"

Polly stops the car with a screech. Then she races away. Ben and Bev run after her.

Now Polly is in the kitchen.

"Look at me!" she says.
"I can juggle six eggs! I'm the
circus star!"

"Please put them down, Polly,"
begs Ben. "This is *not* the
circus!"

Chapter 3
The Show Ends

"Oops!" says Polly as she
zips away.

Ben mops up the mess while
Bev runs after Polly.

"Jump, Kitty," says Polly.
"You're a circus lion. Jump
through the hoop!"

Kitty doesn't want to be a lion,
so Polly flies away.

Polly is worn out! Bev and Ben see Polly pull the cage door shut.

"It looks like Polly has run out of gas," says Ben.

"Goodnight, Polly," says Bev. "Have a good nap."

"Have a good nap," squawks Polly.

Ben and Bev laugh. "Oh, we will!" they say.

Respond to Reading

Retell

Use your own words to retell details in *Polly the Circus Star*.

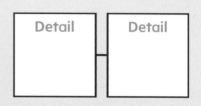

Text Evidence

1. What details tell you what Polly does in the kitchen?

   Key Details: Sequence

2. What does Ben do after Polly zips away? Key Details: Sequence

3. Tell why *Polly the Circus Star* is a fantasy. Genre

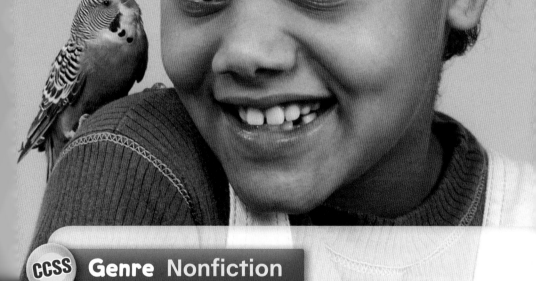

Birds That Talk

Genre Nonfiction

Compare Texts
Read about pet birds that can be trained to speak.

Birds are smart pets. Some of them can learn to speak. Do you want to train your pet bird to speak? Start when your bird is young. Say the same words over and over. Speak clearly and slowly. Be patient. Teaching a bird to speak can take time.

African gray parrot

perch

What a Pet Bird Needs

1. a clean, safe cage with a perch
2. fresh water and the right food
3. exercise time outside its cage
4. to have its nails clipped
5. toys
6. your time and attention

Make Connections
How are real pet birds different
from Polly in *Polly the Circus Star*?

Text to Text

Focus on
Science

Purpose To find out the kinds of things pets need

What to Do

Step 1 Choose a pet you have or would like to have.

Step 2 Make a chart like this one.

My pet is a _____.
My pet needs
  1. _____
  2. _____
  3. _____

Step 3 Fill in the chart with three things the pet needs.

Conclusion Talk about why your pet needs the things you listed.